IODINE

Kristi Lew

53   **127**

I

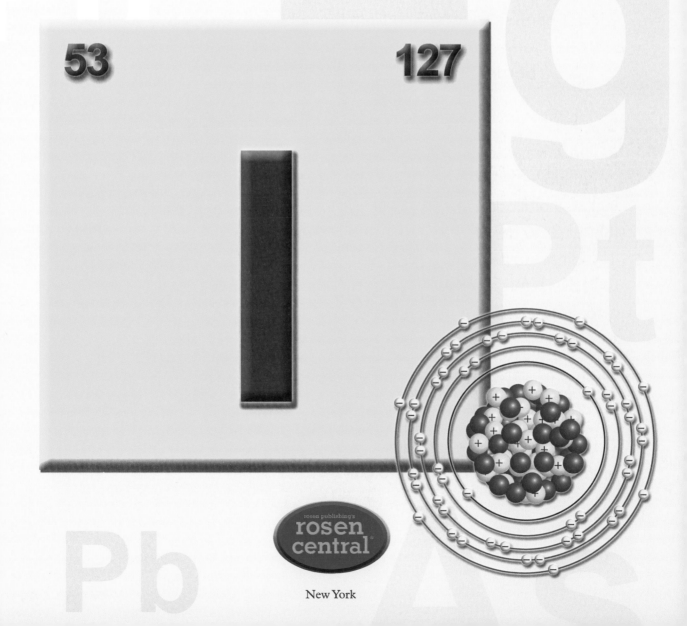

rosen publishing's
rosen central®

New York

To my grandmother, who never failed to paint my cuts and scrapes with iodine solution in an attempt to keep me healthy

Published in 2009 by The Rosen Publishing Group, Inc.
29 East 21st Street, New York, NY 10010

Library of Congress Cataloging-in-Publication Data

Lew, Kristi.
Iodine / Kristi Lew.
    p. cm.—(Understanding the elements of the periodic table)
Includes bibliographical references and index.
ISBN-13: 978-1-4358-5071-2 (library binding)
1. Iodine—Juvenile literature. I. Title.
QD181.I1L54 2009
546'.734—dc22

                                                              2008015691

Manufactured in the United States of America

On the cover: Iodine's square on the periodic table of elements. Inset: the atomic structure of an iodine atom.

Contents

Introduction

Imagine being able to make rain. Many cultures, including ancient Egyptian and Native American cultures, performed ceremonial dances that were designed to do just that. Scientists do not dance to produce rain, but they can make it nevertheless.

How is it possible for people to make rain? One way is to drop a chemical compound called silver iodide (AgI) from an airplane into super-cold clouds. Once the silver iodide is inside a cloud, tiny ice pellets collect on it. Snowflakes begin to form and they get bigger and bigger. When the snowflakes get really big, they become too heavy to stay in the air anymore and they begin to fall to the ground as snow. This process is called cloud seeding.

For the cloud-seeding process to work, the clouds need to contain tiny drops of supercooled water. Supercooled water is water that is below its freezing point but is still in liquid form. Normally, water freezes into a solid below 32° Fahrenheit (0° Celsius), so how is it possible for super-cooled water to exist in liquid form? Water molecules crystallize into solid ice best if there are already other crystals on which to attach. Any little speck of ice, dust, or other chemical can provide a starting place for an ice crystal to grow. In the absence of something to start crystallizing on, however, the supercooled water can remain in liquid form.

Scientists sometimes use airplanes to seed clouds with silver iodide. Ice crystals collect around the chemical and fall to the ground as rain.

Scientists use silver iodide to "seed" clouds because the crystal shape of the chemical is similar to that of ice. The process of starting a crystal is called nucleation. The silver iodide provides a nucleus on which ice crystals can grow. As the ice falls through the air and reaches lower altitudes (gets closer to the surface of Earth) where the temperatures are warmer, it melts and falls as rain.

However, whether cloud seeding actually works is still up for debate in the scientific community. In 2003, the National Academy of Sciences stated that there was no definite scientific evidence to suggest that the process makes it rain when it was not going to do so already. The

American Meteorological Service, on the other hand, maintains that some studies show that rain measurements have gone up as much as 10 percent in some regions due to cloud seeding.

If cloud seeding does indeed work, then it does not always work as predicted. In fact, some people believe that secret cloud-seeding experiments carried out in England in the 1950s led to devastating floods and caused numerous deaths. Were the cloud-seeding experiments responsible for the floods? Or, was it Mother Nature? No one really knows for sure, but one point is certain—when people try to change the weather, the results may not always go as planned.

Chapter One
Iodine in History

Iodine (chemical symbol: I) can be a very useful element. An element is a substance that cannot be broken down into simpler substances through ordinary chemical means, such as by burning or adding acid or electricity. Elements are made up of only one type of atom. Atoms are the smallest units of matter. Iodine is one of the 111 elements that have been discovered and then confirmed by scientists so far (although there are several others waiting to be verified). (See the Periodic Table of Elements on pages 40–41.)

In addition to its application in cloud seeding, iodine and substances that contain it are used to detect and treat cancer, prevent infections, and protect people from radiation in the event of a nuclear accident. None of these beneficial uses of iodine would be possible, however, if it were not for the Napoleonic Wars.

A Shortage of Saltpeter

Iodine was discovered in 1811 by the French chemist Barnard Courtois (1777–1838). At the time of Courtois' discovery, France was engaged in the Napoleonic Wars, a series of wars with other European countries. The Napoleonic Wars were fought until 1815, when the French emperor Napoléon Bonaparte was finally defeated in the Battle of Waterloo.

When the British navy prevented France from getting the saltpeter it needed to make gunpowder during the Napoleonic Wars, the French (including chemist Barnard Courtois) made their own.

To wage his wars, Napoléon needed gunpowder. To make gunpowder, a chemical called saltpeter is required. The scientific name for saltpeter is potassium nitrate (chemical formula: KNO_3). Potassium nitrate is a chemical compound. Chemical compounds are formed when two or more elements are chemically bonded together.

Britain was one of the countries that Napoléon was fighting in the war, and the British did not want him to get the saltpeter he needed. Consequently, the British navy prevented any ships carrying saltpeter from reaching the shores of France. Because France could not get the saltpeter it desired, Courtois (and many others) began to make their own saltpeter.

To do this, Courtois burned the abundant seaweed that could be found in the ocean off the coast of France. When seaweed is burned, its ashes contain the potassium nitrate considered necessary to manufacture gunpowder.

In the process of burning the seaweed to get potassium nitrate, however, other chemical compounds are produced. To eliminate these unwanted compounds, Courtois added sulfuric acid (H_2SO_4) to the seaweed ashes. He did this so that the sulfuric acid would chemically react with the unwanted chemicals and leave behind only the potassium nitrate that he wanted. One day, Courtois added a little too much sulfuric acid to the ashes. To his surprise, a dark purple vapor (gas) appeared. When the violet vapor cooled, lustrous (shiny) dark purple crystals formed. Almost immediately, Courtois realized the substance was likely an element that he had never seen before.

In his spare time, Courtois carried out a few experiments with the new substance. He found that it reacted easily with the elements hydrogen (H) and phosphorous (P), as well as with some metals. It did not react very easily with the elements oxygen (O) or carbon (C), though. Courtois also found that, when mixed with ammonia, the new substance became highly explosive.

Nevertheless, with the war going on, Courtois could not devote much time to experimenting with his new find. Instead, he gave samples of the new substance to the French chemists Charles-Bernard Désormes (1777–1862) and Nicolas Clément (1779–1841), who carried out more systematic experiments with the substance. Courtois also shared samples with Louis-Joseph Gay-Lussac (1778–1850), a French chemist, and André M. Ampère (1775–1836), a French physicist. On November 29, 1813, Désormes and Clément announced the results of their experiments and their suspicions that the substance was a new element. Several days later, Gay-Lussac and Ampère proved that the substance was indeed a

Secret Messages

Iodine can be used to detect the presence of starch (a chemical found in many plants). If starch is there, then a solution of iodine will turn from red-brown to blue-black. Spies can make good use of this property to write secret messages—and so can you!

To make ink that you can use to write a secret message, mix one-half teaspoon (2.5 milliliters) of cornstarch with one-fourth cup (57 ml) of water and stir it vigorously to eliminate any lumps and to make a smooth mixture. Heat the mixture slightly, until it just begins to bubble—about thirty seconds in a microwave should do it—and stir until it is smooth. The mixture will thicken slightly. Dip a cotton swab or pipe cleaner into the starch mixture and use it to write your message on a piece of paper. Let the paper dry.

While the paper is drying, make a solution of iodine by mixing one-half teaspoon (2.5 ml) of iodine tincture (iodine mixed with alcohol) with three tablespoons (44.4 ml) of water. You can get iodine tincture, which is often used to disinfect wounds, from a drug store. Be sure to observe the warnings on the label of iodine tincture: It is toxic, so do not ingest it, and keep it out of your eyes!

To reveal your invisible message, dip a cotton ball or wad of paper towel into the prepared iodine mixture. Gently dab the iodine solution onto the paper containing your secret message. Don't rub, or you might smear the message. Your message will appear in dark purple writing!

[Note: Because iodine is toxic, you should ask an adult to supervise this experiment.]

French chemist Louis-Joseph Gay-Lussac named the new element iode, meaning "violet," because of the deep purple color of its vapor and crystals.

new element. Sir Humphry Davy (1778–1829), an English chemist and physicist, confirmed Gay-Lussac and Ampère's conclusion. Gay-Lussac named the new element iode from the Greek word *iodes*, which means "violet."

Courtois never benefited from his discovery of iodine. In fact, when the Napoleonic Wars ended, the blockade on saltpeter was lifted and Courtois' saltpeter manufacturing business went bankrupt. Courtois died penniless in 1838.

Iodine in Nature

Most of the iodine found in nature is in seaweed. The element is naturally found in seawater in the form of sodium iodide (NaI) and potassium iodide (KI). These salts get concentrated in the seaweed. The most common way to get pure iodine today is by using the same method as Courtois did—burning seaweed.

Pure iodine can also be obtained from natural brines. Brine is very salty water formed when the water of a former ocean starts to evaporate. Over time, these former seas are covered by dirt, and, eventually, the dirt turns to rock that contains pockets of brine. Arkansas and Oklahoma have

In nature, most iodine is found in chemical compounds present in seawater. Pure iodine can be gotten by burning seaweed that has soaked up these compounds.

underground wells of brine that formed in this manner. Today, these wells are mined for iodine. To get pure iodine from the brine, chlorine gas (Cl_2) is bubbled through the brine. Chlorine is more reactive than iodine, and it replaces iodine in the salts. In the process, pure iodine vapor is produced. The iodine vapor is cooled to get pure iodine crystals.

Chapter Two
Inside Iodine

I odine's square on the periodic table of elements is found in row 5, column 17 (or VIIA in an older naming system) on the right-hand side. The periodic table is a very useful tool for chemists. All the elements that have been discovered so far are listed on the periodic table.

The Periodic Table

Today, all of the elements on the periodic table are listed in order of their atomic numbers. However, this has not always been the case. Russian chemist Dmitry Mendeleyev (also spelled Dmitri Mendeleev) (1834–1907) was one of the first scientists to make a periodic table that was widely used. He arranged

Dmitry Mendeleyev developed one of the first widely used periodic tables. Using his table, Mendeleyev was able to correctly predict properties of elements that had not yet been discovered.

the elements known during his time (about sixty elements) in order of their atomic weight. When he did this, Mendeleyev discovered that the properties of the elements in his table exhibited periodic, or regular, patterns. Whenever the regular pattern of properties did not correspond to a known element, Mendeleyev left a blank in his table. He predicted that, one day, elements possessing the correct properties to fill in the blanks of his table would be discovered. In 1875, Mendeleyev was proven to be correct with the discovery of gallium (Ga). His ideas were further confirmed by the discoveries of the elements scandium (Sc) in 1879 and germanium (Ge) in 1886. All three of these elements possessed properties that fit neatly into one of the blanks Mendeleyev had left in his periodic table.

Iodine and the Halogens

Rows on the periodic table are called periods. Columns are called families or groups. Group 17 elements include not only iodine but also fluorine (F), chlorine, bromine (Br), and astatine (At). This group of elements is called the halogen group. Halogens are fairly reactive elements. They react easily with most metals and with some nonmetals as well. Fluorine is the most reactive element in the group. Fluorine reacts so easily that if it is mixed with a compound containing another halogen, it will take the place of that halogen in the compound. Chlorine is the next most reactive halogen, followed by bromine. Iodine is next, and astatine is the least reactive halogen element. All the halogens have a strong, unpleasant odor, and they burn flesh on contact. Except for fluorine, they dissolve a little in water but more in alcohol. Fluorine is so reactive that it does not dissolve in water but reacts with it instead.

As you move down the halogen group on the periodic table, the atoms of the elements get heavier and heavier. Fluorine, the lightest of the

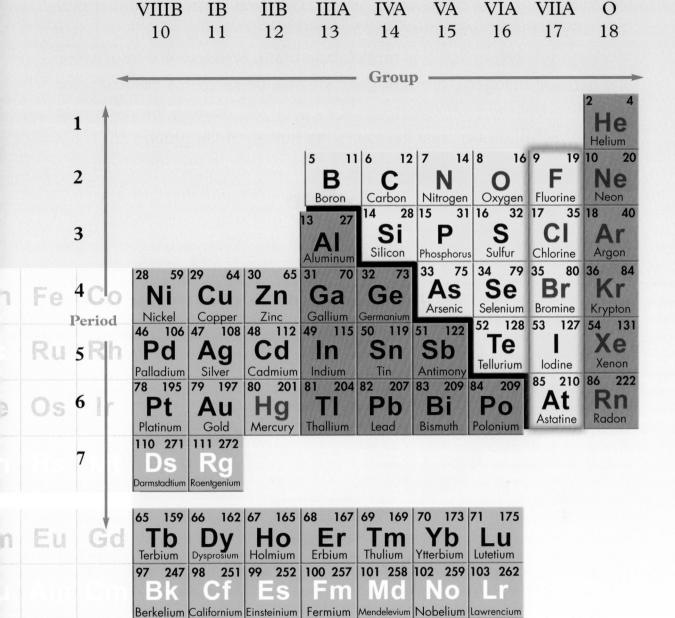

Iodine is on the right-hand side of the periodic table with the other nonmetals. The element, whose symbol is I, is located in period 5, group 17. Group 17 elements are also called halogens. The halogen group is highlighted.

halogens, is a gas at room temperature (about 68°F [20°C]). Even though chlorine weighs almost twice as much as fluorine does, it is also a gas. Bromine, heavier than either fluorine or chlorine, on the other hand, is a dark reddish-brown liquid at room temperature. Both iodine and astatine, the heaviest halogens, are solids. As the size of the atoms increases, the attraction between the atoms becomes stronger, causing the difference in the states of matter from the top to the bottom of the group.

An Inside Look at Iodine

In 1913, Henry Moseley (1887–1915), a British physicist, rearranged Mendeleyev's periodic table when he discovered that an element's properties are determined more by the way its subatomic particles are

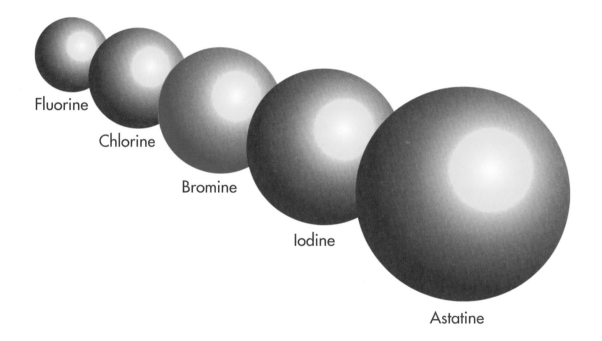

Fluorine

Chlorine

Bromine

Iodine

Astatine

The size of the atoms increases as you move down the halogen group on the periodic table. Fluorine has the shortest atomic radius, while astatine has the longest. Fluorine atoms have nine electrons surrounding their nuclei, bromine atoms have thirty-five, and astatine atoms have eighty-five.

arranged within its atoms than by its atomic weight. Every atom is made up of subatomic particles (subatomic means smaller than an atom). There are three types of subatomic particles: protons, neutrons, and electrons.

Moseley rearranged the periodic table so that the elements were in order by atomic number. The atomic number of an element is equal to the number of protons in the element's atoms. Iodine's atomic number, for example, is 53. That means that every iodine atom contains fifty-three protons. If an atom contains any other number of protons, then it is not an atom of iodine but an atom of some other element. If the atom has fifty-two protons, for example, then it is an atom of tellurium (Te). An atom with fifty-four protons is an atom of xenon (Xe).

Sublimation

Objects or substances usually exist in one of the three most common states of matter: solid, liquid, or gas. Generally, if a solid is heated, it melts and turns into a liquid. In turn, a liquid that is heated evaporates and becomes a gas. Iodine, however, is different. When iodine is heated, it does not melt. Instead, it changes directly from a solid to a gas. The process of changing from a solid to a gas, entirely bypassing the liquid stage, is called sublimation.

Heating iodine, a blackish solid at room temperature, changes it to a purple gas.

Protons are found in the nucleus, or center, of an atom. Neutrons, another type of subatomic particle, are also found in the nucleus. Together, the protons and neutrons of an atom make up most of an atom's weight. A proton weighs 1.67×10^{-27} kilograms (or 0.000 000 000 000 000 000 000 001 67 grams). This number is so small that it is hard to work with. Instead, chemists use a unit of weight called an atomic mass unit (amu). An atomic mass unit is equal to 1.67×10^{-27} kilograms. Therefore, a proton weighs 1 amu. That number is much easier to work with! A neutron also weighs 1 amu. All the weights of the elements on a periodic table are listed in atomic mass units. The atomic weight of iodine, for example, is listed as 127 amu. If an atom of iodine has fifty-three protons and a weight of 127 amu, then the atom must have 74 neutrons (because $74 + 53 = 127$).

Electrons, the third type of subatomic particle, weigh much less than protons and neutrons. The weight of an electron is only 1/2000 of the weight of a proton. Unlike protons and neutrons, electrons are found outside of the nucleus. They move around the nucleus in energy levels, or shells. Protons and electrons both have electrical charges. A proton has a positive charge, and an electron has a negative charge. Neutrons do not have a charge; they are neutral.

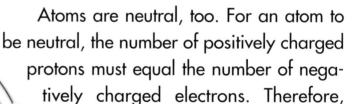

Atoms are neutral, too. For an atom to be neutral, the number of positively charged protons must equal the number of negatively charged electrons. Therefore, because an iodine atom contains fifty-three protons, it must also have fifty-three electrons.

Every iodine atom has fifty-three protons in its nucleus and fifty-three electrons moving around the outside of the nucleus on five energy levels.

Iodine Snapshot

Chemical Symbol:	I
Classification:	Nonmetal; halogen
Properties:	Bluish-black shiny solid, which sublimes into a purple gas
Discovered By:	Barnard Courtois in 1811
Atomic Number:	53
Atomic Weight:	127 atomic mass units (amu)
Protons:	53
Electrons:	53
Neutrons:	74
State of Matter at 68°F (20°C):	Solid
Melting Point:	236.7°F (113.7°C)
Boiling Point:	364.0°F (184.4°C)
Commonly Found:	In seaweed and brine

Valence Electrons

An iodine atom's electrons are arranged around its nucleus in five energy levels. The outermost (highest) energy level contains seven electrons. Electrons in an atom's highest energy level are called valence electrons. Atoms lose, gain, or share valence electrons when forming a chemical bond with other atoms. Chemists use a rule of thumb called the octet rule, which says that an atom will lose, gain, or share enough electrons to obtain eight electrons in its highest energy level.

Because an iodine atom possesses seven electrons in its highest energy level, it only needs to gain or share one electron to be stable.

Iodine is a diatomic element. The atoms of diatomic elements are always found in pairs. There are seven naturally occurring diatomic elements: hydrogen, oxygen, nitrogen, fluorine, chlorine, bromine, and iodine.

For this reason, iodine atoms are never found alone. Instead, in the element two iodine atoms form a bond with each other and share a valence electron. That way, both iodine atoms have eight valence electrons. As a result, the chemical formula for the element iodine, when it is not in a chemical compound with another element, is written as I_2. Elements that exist as two atoms bonded together are called diatomic elements. Iodine is not the only diatomic element. The others are hydrogen (H_2), oxygen (O_2), nitrogen (N_2), fluorine (F_2), chlorine (Cl_2), and bromine (Br_2).

Writing secret messages is not the only way in which iodine can be of use to people. Iodine can be a helpful substance to have around the science laboratory and in the hospital, too.

Iodine and the Biology Laboratory

The same principle that allowed the starch-laden invisible ink to show up when iodine came into contact with it can be of use to biologists as well as spies. Remember that when iodine is added to a starch, it turns a deep blue-black color. Starch is a chemical found in many types of plants. Plants use the chemical to store their food. Some plants such as potatoes, rice, wheat, and corn are especially rich in starch. Biologists can use iodine to test for the presence of starch in food and other items.

Iodine Identifies Bacteria

Iodine can also help a biologist identify types of bacteria. Bacteria are often classified according to two major categories—those that react with Gram stain and those that do not. Bacteria that react with Gram stain are called Gram-positive bacteria. Ones that don't are called Gram-negative bacteria. Gram staining is named for Hans Christian Gram (1853–1938),

Iodine can be used to test for the presence of starch. The darker the blue-black color, the more starch there is in the sample. In this example, the test tube at the far left has 100 times more starch than that found in the test tube at the far right.

the Danish scientist who developed the method in 1884. Gram staining is the first step in identifying a particular strain of bacteria.

To stain bacteria with Gram stain requires several steps. The specimen (sputum, urine, or other bodily fluid suspected of containing bacteria) is first spread thinly over a microscope slide. The slide is then flooded with a stain called crystal violet. This tints all bacteria purple. A solution of potassium iodide (KI), called Gram's iodine, is then added to the slide. The iodine solution is not a dye but a mordant. A mordant sets, or fixes, a dye. In this case, the iodine solution sets the crystal violet dye in the cell wall of some of the bacterial cells but not in others. The cells are then treated with an alcohol solution. The alcohol solution takes the color out of the bacterial cells that did not react with the Gram's iodine.

Gram-positive bacteria will not lose their purple color because their cell walls absorb the dye and Gram's iodine sets the dye in their cell walls. The cell walls of Gram-negative bacteria, on the other hand, do not absorb the iodine-dye molecules. When alcohol is applied to Gram-negative bacteria, it becomes colorless. Finally, a counter stain is added to the microscope slide. The counter stain is a red dye. When it is added to the slide, it turns the colorless Gram-negative bacteria bright pink or red, while the Gram-positive bacteria remain dark purple.

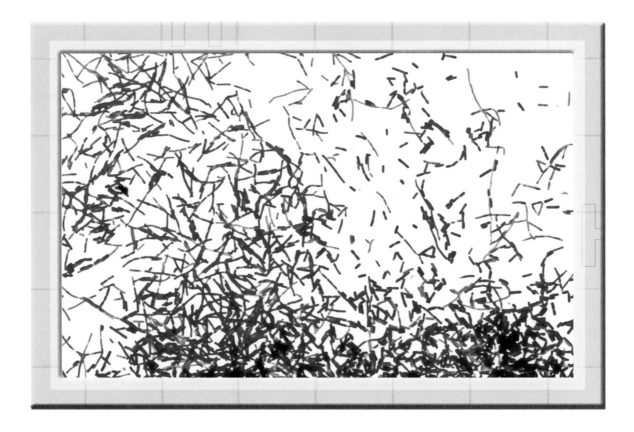

This microscopic image shows bacteria after being exposed to Gram's iodine in a Gram-staining procedure. Gram-positive bacteria are dark purple-colored. Gram-negative bacteria, on the other hand, appear pink. Researchers use Gram stain to help them classify bacteria forms and sizes.

Even though biologists today have more sophisticated ways to identify the exact type of bacteria, the Gram stain test still persists because it is fast. All the modern techniques require time for the bacteria to grow in culture (in a Petri dish in the laboratory). The Gram stain test, on the other hand, can provide a doctor with results in just a few minutes. It can be performed on samples taken from a patient right in the doctor's office, and it allows the doctor to give preventative medicine quickly. This immediate treatment could mean the difference between life and death in diseases such as bacterial meningitis and pneumonia, which require fast action by physicians to prevent a patient from getting sicker.

Iodine Identifies a Fake

Have you ever seen a bank teller or store clerk swipe a pen that looks like a highlighter over a banknote (currency)? That person was using a pen that can detect counterfeit bills. Most paper is made of starch-containing wood fibers. Banknotes made by the U.S. Department of the Treasury are specially treated to remove all traces of starch.

Special pens contain iodine to detect counterfeit bills. When the pen is swiped over a genuine bill, the streak is yellow or colorless. If counterfeiters have printed a fake bill on paper that contains starch, the streak left by the pen turns dark purple or black.

Store clerks sometimes use pens that contain iodine to help them detect counterfeit currency.

Iodine Identifies Fat

Biologists are not the only scientists who use iodine in the laboratory. Chemists use it, too. One of the ways iodine is used in chemistry is to determine if a fat is saturated or unsaturated.

Fats are substances made up of carbon, hydrogen, and oxygen. In some fats, the carbon atoms are all chemically bonded to one another with single chemical bonds. The carbon atoms in these fats are also bonded to as many hydrogen atoms as possible. Therefore, fats with single chemical bonds between each carbon atom are called saturated fats because they are saturated with (full of) hydrogen atoms.

When iodine is added to an unsaturated fat, it breaks apart carbon-carbon double bonds and iodine atoms attach to the carbon atoms.

However, not all fats have single bonds between their carbon atoms. The carbon atoms in some fats are bonded to one another with double bonds. Carbon-carbon double bonds do not leave as much room in the fat molecule for hydrogen atoms. Therefore, fats that contain double bonds do not contain all the hydrogen that is possible. This type of fat is called unsaturated.

When iodine is added to an unsaturated fat, the carbon-carbon double bonds are broken and iodine atoms bond to the carbon atoms. The more double bonds that are in the fat, the more iodine bonds to it. The number of grams of iodine that bond to 100 grams (3.5 ounces) of a chemical substance is called its iodine number or iodine value. The more unsaturated a fat is, the higher its iodine number. Saturated fats, on the other hand, have a low iodine number.

Iodine Kills and Heals

Doctors have used iodine as an antiseptic for more than 150 years. An antiseptic (also called a germicide) is a substance that can slow or stop the growth of bacteria and other microorganisms. Antiseptics are used to prevent infection. However, this is not the only use for iodine in the medical profession. Doctors can also use iodine to detect and treat thyroid cancer.

To determine whether someone has thyroid cancer or not, a doctor may order a test called a thyroid scan. During this test, the patient swallows a pill that contains a radioactive isotope of iodine. An isotope is a form of an element that has a particular number of neutrons. One iodine isotope used to diagnose and treat thyroid cancer is iodine-131. The number after the element's name identifies the weight of the isotope. Iodine-131 has an atomic weight of 131 amu. Because iodine-131 must have fifty-three protons (or it would not be iodine; it would be some other element), this isotope must have seventy-eight neutrons.

The nucleus of iodine-131, unlike that of the usual iodine-127, is unstable. It breaks down, giving off radiation. Radiation is energy that

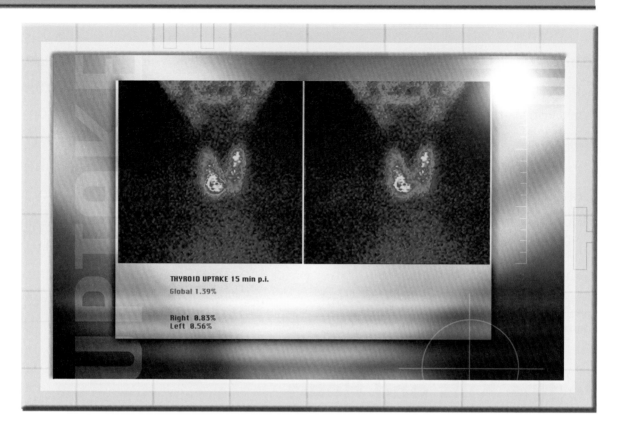

THYROID UPTAKE 15 min p.i.
Global 1.39%

Right 0.83%
Left 0.56%

Doctors can use iodine-131 to determine how a patient's thyroid gland is functioning. In these pictures, the thyroid gland appears brighter and larger on the left side of each image, showing that there is more activity.

is transmitted in the form of rays, waves, or particles. The thyroid gland absorbs and concentrates iodine in the body, and it does this with iodine-131, too. Doctors can use special medical equipment to detect the radiation given off by the radioactive iodine as it is taken up by the thyroid gland during the scan. This procedure allows doctors to see if the thyroid gland is functioning properly.

Doctors use radioactive iodine not only to diagnose thyroid cancer but also to treat it. When iodine-131 is taken up by the thyroid gland, the radiation it emits can destroy cancer cells. Iodine-131 is a form of chemotherapy (using chemicals to treat cancer). Because other cells in the body do not absorb iodine, they are unaffected by the radiation.

Chapter Four
Iodine in Compounds

When iodine is chemically bonded to other elements in chemical compounds, the compounds can be extremely useful as well.

Iodine in Photography

Cloud seeding is not the only use for the chemical compound silver iodide. Photographers use it, too (photographers who still use film, that is). Almost 170 years ago, the first practical photographs, called daguerreotypes, used plates covered in silver iodide to capture

A daguerreotype is an early form of photography. Iodine fumes were used with a silver plate to create a light-sensitive compound for producing pictures. Made in the 1840s by Nicholas Shepherd, this daguerreotype is believed to be one of the earliest images of Abraham Lincoln.

photographs. Silver iodide is a light-sensitive chemical. When it is exposed to light, a chemical reaction occurs that splits the silver iodide into silver (Ag) atoms and iodine atoms. The free silver atoms produce a dark area on the section of film that was exposed to the light. The areas not exposed to light remain white. This produces a negative image that can then be reversed into a photograph.

Iodine Detects Ozone

Another iodine compound, called potassium iodide (KI), can detect ozone. Ozone is a gas whose molecules contain three oxygen atoms chemically bonded together. The chemical formula for ozone is O_3. Ozone is much more reactive than the ordinary diatomic oxygen that is found in air.

Ozone in the lowest level of the atmosphere, the troposphere, where people live and breathe, can be a problem. It can harm humans, plants,

Disinfecting Water

Because iodine is an antiseptic, it can be used to disinfect drinking water in an emergency situation. Commercially prepared iodine tablets contain iodine compounds and are often used by campers and military personnel to prepare safe drinking water. The iodine compounds kill harmful bacteria in the water when boiling is not possible. If no iodine tablets are available, then tincture of iodine (a solution of iodine in alcohol, which is available in drug stores) can be used instead. Too much iodine can be toxic, however. Only five drops of iodine tincture is needed for about one quart (1 liter) of clear water. If the water is cloudy, however, then adding ten drops of iodine tincture before allowing the water to settle is recommended.

and animals and is, therefore, considered a pollutant. However, in the stratosphere, the level of Earth's atmosphere just above the troposphere, ozone is beneficial. It keeps a majority of the sun's ultraviolet (UV) rays from reaching Earth's surface, where they would harm plants and animals.

Ozone was discovered more than one hundred years ago by German chemist Christian Frederick Schönbein (1799–1868). Schönbein did not just discover ozone. He also developed a test to detect the chemical. Schönbein's test paper is made by soaking a piece of paper in a paste of potassium iodide, cornstarch, and water. In the presence of ozone, the potassium iodide changes into pure iodine. The iodine reacts with the starch in the paper producing a purplish-black color. The darker purple the paper turns, the more ozone is present in the air.

Other Ideal Uses of Iodine

Iodine can be used in other ways as well. For example, it is used to set dyes and inks in fabric and paper. In these processes, the iodine acts as a mordant, just as it does during Gram staining of bacteria.

Iodine compounds are also used to help doctors take better X-rays. X-ray images are great for distinguishing bone from soft tissue, but telling one soft tissue (such as an organ, for example) from another using an X-ray is much more difficult. Compounds that contain iodine, though, are easily taken up by organs and tissues in the body, especially those with a high blood flow such as cancerous tumors. Iodine scatters X-rays more effectively than human soft tissue does. Scattering the X-rays makes the parts of the body that take up iodine show up better on the X-ray film. Tissues that absorb a lot of the iodine compounds show up as white on the X-ray.

The U.S. armed forces also utilize compounds that contain iodine. In fact, the military invented a weapon in 1977 called the chemical oxygen iodine laser (COIL). Inside a COIL weapon, a chemical reaction between chlorine and hydrogen peroxide (H_2O_2) creates enough energy to excite oxygen atoms. An excited atom is one that has more energy than it normally possesses. The oxygen atoms transfer their energy to iodine atoms. This transfer of energy excites the iodine atoms. The energy contained in the excited iodine atoms is used to produce a laser beam. The laser beam is designed to shoot down ballistic missiles launched at the United States from a hostile country.

Iodized Salt

Too much iodine can be toxic to the human body, but a little bit of iodine is needed for the body to function properly. Without enough iodine, the

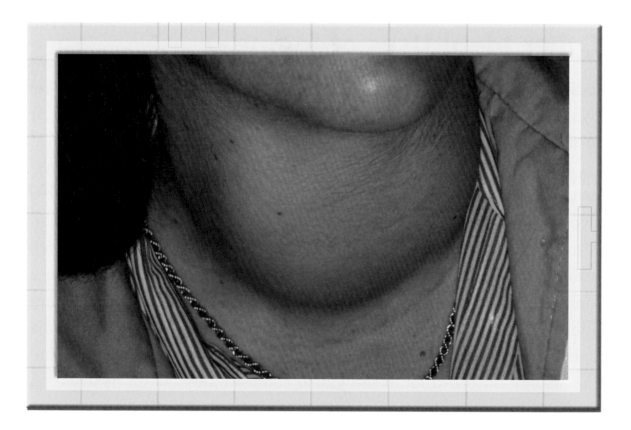

Not getting enough iodine in the food you eat can cause the thyroid gland to swell. A swollen neck caused by an enlarged thyroid gland is called a goiter.

thyroid gland cannot do its job. Often, the thyroid glands of people who do not get enough iodine swell. A swelling of the neck (where the thyroid gland is located) is called a goiter. Goiters used to be a big problem in the United States. However, the addition of potassium iodide to table salt has greatly reduced the occurrence of goiters in the general population.

Salt that contains potassium iodide is called iodized salt. Many officials see the use of iodized salt as one of the best public health interventions ever attempted. In the United States, only table salt is iodized. Salt that is added to canned food, fast food, and other processed foods does not contain iodine.

In 2006, Canadian researcher Stephen A. Hoption Cann of the University of British Columbia in Vancouver became concerned about an apparent increase in iodine deficiency in North Americans. Some health studies show that in the 1970s, only about one in forty Americans had a slight-to-moderate iodine deficiency. Those same studies conducted in the 1990s, however, showed that one in nine Americans suffered from an iodine deficiency.

Why would the incidence of iodine deficiency go up? Cann believes that it is possibly due to the popularity of low-sodium diets. While avoiding the use of table salt is good for people's blood pressure, it may be increasing the number of people who are iodine deficient. Another scientific study proposed a different reason for the increase in iodine deficiency in Americans. That study showed that the iodine content in iodized salt in the United States varies widely from product to product. Therefore, even people who are eating iodized table salt may not be getting as much iodine in their diets as they need.

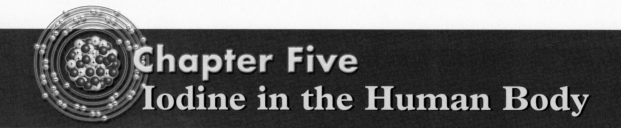

Chapter Five
Iodine in the Human Body

It is important that people get enough iodine in their diets because the body needs iodine for the proper growth, development, and functioning of the brain and body. Iodine is used by the thyroid gland to make a hormone called thyroxin. Thyroxin controls everything from how often the heart beats to the body's metabolism (how fast it burns calories).

Iodine Deficiency

Iodine deficiency can be especially harmful in unborn babies and young children because the brain is developing quickly at these stages of life. Iodine deficiency can cause mental retardation or death in newborns and infants. Though iodine deficiency is relatively rare in the United States today, it affects about 35 percent of children in developing countries. However, iodine deficiency is considered a preventable cause of mental retardation and brain damage.

Along with goiters, mental retardation, and stunted growth, iodine deficiency can also result in hypothyroidism. Hypothyroidism occurs when the thyroid gland does not produce enough hormones. Symptoms of hypothyroidism include tiredness, weight gain, and extreme sleepiness. If the condition is not diagnosed, then it can get worse. In severe cases,

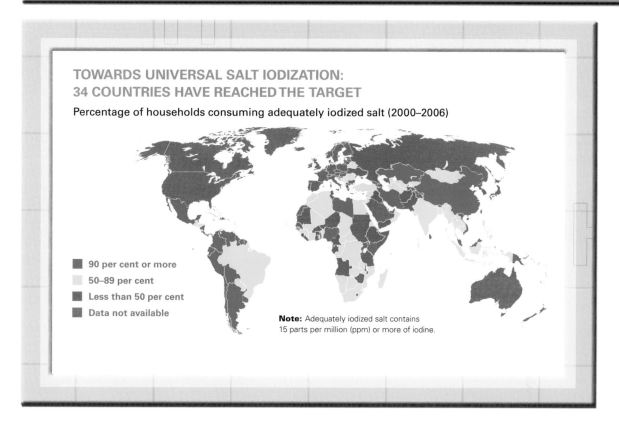

**TOWARDS UNIVERSAL SALT IODIZATION:
34 COUNTRIES HAVE REACHED THE TARGET**

Percentage of households consuming adequately iodized salt (2000–2006)

- ■ 90 per cent or more
- ■ 50–89 per cent
- ■ Less than 50 per cent
- ■ Data not available

Note: Adequately iodized salt contains 15 parts per million (ppm) or more of iodine.

The World Health Organization (WHO) is just one agency working hard to eliminate iodine deficiency globally by supplying iodized salt to people who do not get enough iodine in their daily diet.

hypothyroidism can cause an enlarged heart (because the heart muscle grows bigger to try to do its job), slowing of the heart rate (the rate the heart beats per minute), and even heart failure.

Iodine in Food

Areas of the world far from the coasts tend to have higher rates of iodine deficiency, especially if people do not have access to iodized salt. Salt does not necessarily have to be added to food for people to get enough iodine in their diets, however. Some foods from the sea such as seafood and seaweed naturally contain iodine. Foods grown in iodine-rich soil

Seafood and seaweed are good sources of dietary iodine. Sushi is often prepared by wrapping seafood, rice, and vegetables in seaweed.

and dairy products (if the cows are eating grass grown in iodine-rich soil) contain iodine, too. Yet, food grown at high altitudes (far from the sea) can be iodine deficient because of iodine-poor soil.

People need to eat iodine-containing food regularly, however, because only the amount needed by the thyroid gland to make sufficient amounts of thyroxin is absorbed by the body at any one time. Excess iodine is not stored. Although iodine is necessary for the proper functioning of the body, it is not required in large amounts. If a person's body weight is divided by 2,500,000, then the result is about the weight of iodine in his or her body. For most people, it works out to be about the size of a pinhead.

Nuclear Accident

The iodine-containing compounds potassium iodide and potassium iodate (KIO_3) can play a different role in keeping people healthy, especially people who live near nuclear power plants. In the event of a nuclear accident, people who live near a malfunctioning nuclear power plant can be given potassium iodide or potassium iodate pills to protect them from the radioactive iodine-131 that is released by the power plant's reactors.

Although iodine-131 has a relatively short half-life (about eight days), the radioisotope is a danger because it becomes concentrated in only one spot in the body—the thyroid gland. This puts people who have been exposed to high doses of iodine-131 at risk for developing thyroid cancer.

One of the worst nuclear disasters the world has ever seen occurred on April 26, 1986, when one of the reactors at the Chernobyl nuclear power plant in the former Soviet republic of the Ukraine exploded. This explosion sent radioactive material into the air for ten days. Millions of people were exposed to radiation. Since the accident, the number of cases of thyroid cancer in children has skyrocketed. Before the accident, doctors diagnosed about twelve cases of childhood thyroid cancer per year. For the five-year period following the Chernobyl accident, though, the number of childhood thyroid cancer cases went up an average of twenty-two cases per year (almost double). Between 1991 and 1995, that number went up again to an average of sixty-three cases each year. By 1997, the number of cases had soared to seventy-three per year (more than six times the average before the accident occurred). Children who were under the age of five, even those who were still in their mothers' wombs at the time of the accident, seem to be the age group that was most affected.

After the Chernobyl accident, the Soviet government gave out potassium iodide pills to anyone living within 30 miles (48.3 kilometers) of the disaster site. Unfortunately, the radiation spread much farther than 30 miles. Potassium iodide or iodate pills work by flooding the thyroid gland with non-radioactive iodine. Because the thyroid only takes up the amount of iodine that it needs, the iodine-containing pills prevent the thyroid from absorbing the radioactive iodine-131. In order for the pills to work, they must be taken within several hours of an accident. The pills do not protect people from any other type of radiation being emitted by the nuclear power plant.

At one time, the U.S. government distributed potassium iodide pills to anyone, especially to pregnant or nursing women and young children, who lived near a nuclear reactor in case of an accident or terrorist attack. According to a January 2008 *USA Today* news report, however, the

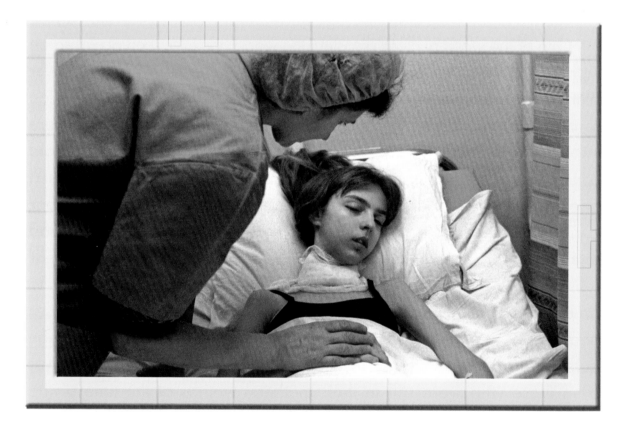

The number of thyroid cancer cases increased dramatically in the Ukraine following the explosion of the Chernobyl nuclear power plant there in 1986. This teen is recuperating from thyroid cancer surgery in Kiev, Ukraine, almost twenty years after the accident.

administration of President George W. Bush discontinued the anti-radiation pill program. Some of the reasons given by federal officials were that the pills offered little protection to people who lived more than 10 miles (16.1 km) from a nuclear plant, that evacuation and protection from contamination were more effective methods to prevent cancer, and that the distribution of pills might damage public confidence in the safety of the nuclear plants.

Luckily, thyroid cancer, when caught before the cancer has had a chance to spread to other parts of the body, is curable by removing the diseased thyroid gland. Patients who have had their thyroid gland removed must take medicine for the rest of their lives to replace their missing thyroid hormones. Most of the children who were diagnosed with thyroid cancer after the Chernobyl accident survived their battle with cancer.

From protecting people from dangerous radiation and bacteria, to detecting high levels of ozone and exposing counterfeiters, iodine certainly is a handy element to have around!

The Periodic Table of Elements

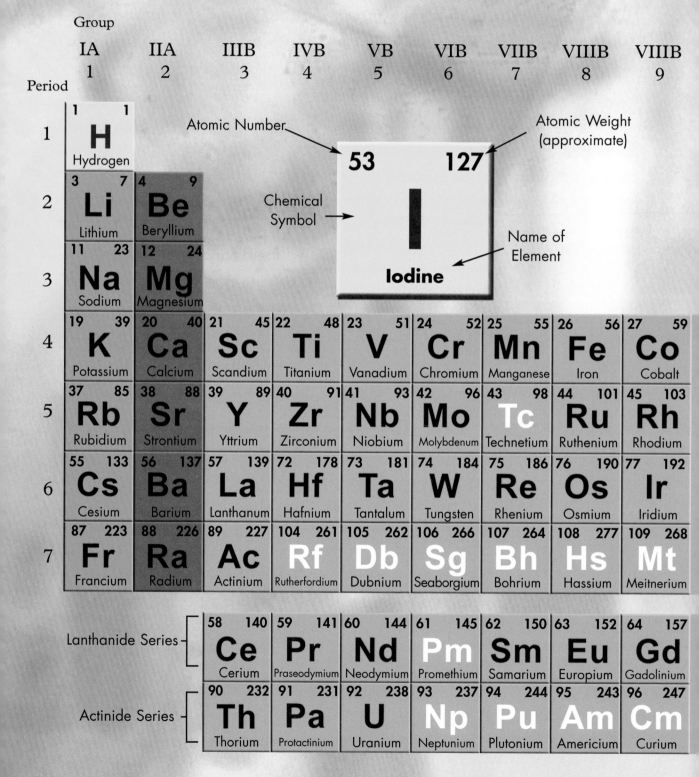

Group

Period	IA 1	IIA 2	IIIB 3	IVB 4	VB 5	VIB 6	VIIB 7	VIIIB 8	VIIIB 9
1	1 1 **H** Hydrogen								
2	3 7 **Li** Lithium	4 9 **Be** Beryllium							
3	11 23 **Na** Sodium	12 24 **Mg** Magnesium							
4	19 39 **K** Potassium	20 40 **Ca** Calcium	21 45 **Sc** Scandium	22 48 **Ti** Titanium	23 51 **V** Vanadium	24 52 **Cr** Chromium	25 55 **Mn** Manganese	26 56 **Fe** Iron	27 59 **Co** Cobalt
5	37 85 **Rb** Rubidium	38 88 **Sr** Strontium	39 89 **Y** Yttrium	40 91 **Zr** Zirconium	41 93 **Nb** Niobium	42 96 **Mo** Molybdenum	43 98 **Tc** Technetium	44 101 **Ru** Ruthenium	45 103 **Rh** Rhodium
6	55 133 **Cs** Cesium	56 137 **Ba** Barium	57 139 **La** Lanthanum	72 178 **Hf** Hafnium	73 181 **Ta** Tantalum	74 184 **W** Tungsten	75 186 **Re** Rhenium	76 190 **Os** Osmium	77 192 **Ir** Iridium
7	87 223 **Fr** Francium	88 226 **Ra** Radium	89 227 **Ac** Actinium	104 261 **Rf** Rutherfordium	105 262 **Db** Dubnium	106 266 **Sg** Seaborgium	107 264 **Bh** Bohrium	108 277 **Hs** Hassium	109 268 **Mt** Meitnerium

Atomic Number

Atomic Weight (approximate)

53 127

I

Iodine

Chemical Symbol

Name of Element

Lanthanide Series	58 140 **Ce** Cerium	59 141 **Pr** Praseodymium	60 144 **Nd** Neodymium	61 145 **Pm** Promethium	62 150 **Sm** Samarium	63 152 **Eu** Europium	64 157 **Gd** Gadolinium
Actinide Series	90 232 **Th** Thorium	91 231 **Pa** Protactinium	92 238 **U** Uranium	93 237 **Np** Neptunium	94 244 **Pu** Plutonium	95 243 **Am** Americium	96 247 **Cm** Curium

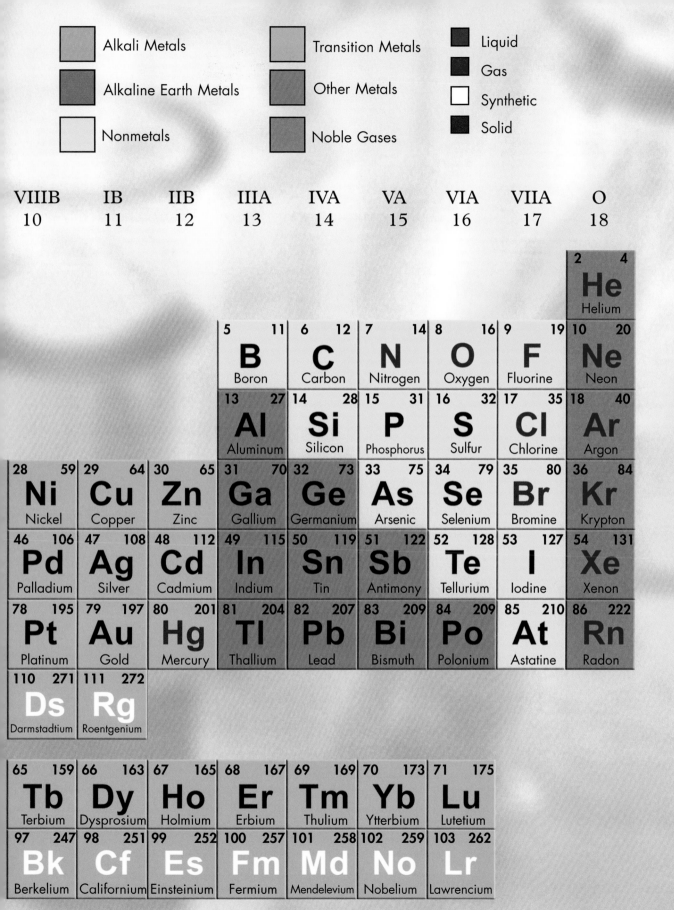

Legend

- Alkali Metals
- Alkaline Earth Metals
- Nonmetals
- Transition Metals
- Other Metals
- Noble Gases
- Liquid
- Gas
- Synthetic
- Solid

VIIIB	IB	IIB	IIIA	IVA	VA	VIA	VIIA	O
10	11	12	13	14	15	16	17	18

								2 4 **He** Helium
			5 11 **B** Boron	6 12 **C** Carbon	7 14 **N** Nitrogen	8 16 **O** Oxygen	9 19 **F** Fluorine	10 20 **Ne** Neon
			13 27 **Al** Aluminum	14 28 **Si** Silicon	15 31 **P** Phosphorus	16 32 **S** Sulfur	17 35 **Cl** Chlorine	18 40 **Ar** Argon
28 59 **Ni** Nickel	29 64 **Cu** Copper	30 65 **Zn** Zinc	31 70 **Ga** Gallium	32 73 **Ge** Germanium	33 75 **As** Arsenic	34 79 **Se** Selenium	35 80 **Br** Bromine	36 84 **Kr** Krypton
46 106 **Pd** Palladium	47 108 **Ag** Silver	48 112 **Cd** Cadmium	49 115 **In** Indium	50 119 **Sn** Tin	51 122 **Sb** Antimony	52 128 **Te** Tellurium	53 127 **I** Iodine	54 131 **Xe** Xenon
78 195 **Pt** Platinum	79 197 **Au** Gold	80 201 **Hg** Mercury	81 204 **Tl** Thallium	82 207 **Pb** Lead	83 209 **Bi** Bismuth	84 209 **Po** Polonium	85 210 **At** Astatine	86 222 **Rn** Radon
110 271 **Ds** Darmstadtium	111 272 **Rg** Roentgenium							

65 159 **Tb** Terbium	66 163 **Dy** Dysprosium	67 165 **Ho** Holmium	68 167 **Er** Erbium	69 169 **Tm** Thulium	70 173 **Yb** Ytterbium	71 175 **Lu** Lutetium
97 247 **Bk** Berkelium	98 251 **Cf** Californium	99 252 **Es** Einsteinium	100 257 **Fm** Fermium	101 258 **Md** Mendelevium	102 259 **No** Nobelium	103 262 **Lr** Lawrencium

Glossary

brine Very salty water formed by the evaporation of ocean water.

compound A substance that contains two or more elements chemically bonded together.

diatomic element Elements whose molecules contain two atoms bonded together (H_2, O_2, N_2, F_2, Cl_2, Br_2, and I_2).

electron A negatively charged subatomic particle that fills most of the space in an atom.

element A substance that cannot be broken down into simpler substances through ordinary chemical means.

goiter Swelling of the neck caused by an iodine deficiency.

halogens The group of elements on the periodic chart that contains fluorine, chlorine, bromine, iodine, and astatine.

isotope A form of an element that has a particular number of neutrons.

mordant A chemical that fixes a dye in or on a substance by combining with the dye to form an insoluble compound.

neutron An uncharged subatomic particle found in the nucleus of an atom.

nucleus The tiny core of an atom made up of protons and (usually) neutrons and that contains most of the atom's mass.

octet rule A principle that states that an atom will lose, gain, or share enough electrons to obtain eight electrons in its highest energy level.

proton A positively charged subatomic particle found in the nucleus of an atom.

sublimation The process of changing from a solid directly to a gas, bypassing the liquid stage.

valence electrons Electrons in an atom's highest energy level that are involved in bonding between atoms.

Iodine Network
180 Elgin Street, Suite 1000
Ottawa, ON K2P 2K3
Canada
(613) 782-6812
Web site: http://www.iodinenetwork.net
The Iodine Network is dedicated to providing iodized salt to all nations
  in an effort to combat iodine deficiency worldwide.

World Health Organization (WHO)
Avenue Appia 20
CH - 1211 Geneva 27
Switzerland
+41 22 791 2111
Web site: http://www.who.int/en
The World Health Organization is the agency in the United Nations
  that is concerned with issues, including iodine deficiency, that affect
  public health.

Web Sites

Due to the changing nature of Internet links, Rosen Publishing has
developed an online list of Web sites related to the subject of this book.
This site is updated regularly. Please use this link to access the list:

http://www.rosenlinks.com/uept/iodi

For Further Reading

Barber, Ian. *Sorting the Elements: The Periodic Table at Work*. Vero Beach, FL: Rourke Publishing, 2008.

Buckingham, Alan. *Photography*. New York, NY: DK Publishing, Inc., 2004.

Claybourne, Anna. *The Nature of Matter*. Pleasantville, NY: Gareth Stevens, 2007.

Gray, Leon. *Iodine*. New York, NY: Benchmark Books, 2005.

Ingram, W. Scott. *The Chernobyl Nuclear Disaster* (Environmental Disasters Series). New York, NY: Facts On File, Inc., 2005

Jerome, Kate Boehm. *Atomic Universe: The Quest to Discover Radioactivity*. Washington, DC: National Geographic Society, 2006.

Mayell, Mark. *Nuclear Accidents*. Detroit, MI: Gale Group, 2003.

Morgan, Sally. *Ozone Hole*. North Mankato, MN: Sea to Sea Publications, 2007.

Morris, Neil. *Salt*. North Mankato, MN: Smart Apple Media, 2006.

Nardo, Don. *Atoms*. San Diego, CA: Kidhaven Press, 2002.

Parker, Steve. *Hormones: Injury, Illness and Health*. Minneapolis, MN: Tandem Library Books, 2003.

Powell, Jillian. *Fats for a Healthy Body*. Chicago, IL: Heinemann, 2003.

Robinson, Tom. *Everything Kids' Magical Science Experiments Book*. Avon, MA: Adams Media Corporation, 2007.

Bibliography

BBC News Online. "Rain-Making Link to Killer Floods." August 30, 2001. Retrieved February 21, 2008 (http://news.bbc.co.uk/2/hi/uk_news/1516880.stm).

Cann, Stephen A. Hoption. "Hypothesis: Dietary Iodine Intake in the Etiology of Cardiovascular Disease." *Journal of the American College of Nutrition*, Vol. 25, No. 1, 2006, pp. 1–11.

Casey, Linda. "How to Make Invisible Ink." Whistler Elementary School. Retrieved February 22, 2008 (http://www.iit.edu/~smile/ch9602.html).

Emsley, John. *Nature's Building Blocks: An A–Z Guide to the Elements.* New York, NY: Oxford University Press, 2001.

Federation of American Scientists. "Airborne Laser." December 2, 2005. Retrieved February 23, 2008 (http://www.fas.org/spp/starwars/program/abl.htm).

Hall, Mimi. "U.S. Scraps Plan for Anti-Radiation Pills." USAToday.com, January 28, 2008. Retrieved April 2, 2008 (http://www/usatoday.com/news/nation/2008-01-28-nuclear-pills_N.htm).

Harvard Health Letter. "In Brief; Is There a Downside to Low-Sodium Diets?" June 2006. Retrieved January 30, 2008 (http://find.galegroup.com/itx/start.do?prodId=EAIM).

International Wellness Directory. "The History of Iodine." Retrieved February 22, 2008 (http://www.mnwelldir.org/docs/history/iodine.htm).

Loyola University Health System. "Gram Stain Technique." Retrieved February 23, 2008 (http://www.meddean.luc.edu/lumen/DeptWebs/microbio/med/gram/tech.htm).

Mayo Foundation for Medical Education and Research. "X-Ray." December 20, 2007. Retrieved February 23, 2008 (http://www.mayoclinic.com/health/x-ray/FL00064).

McNeil, Donald G., Jr. "In Raising the World's I.Q., the Secret's in the Salt." *New York Times*, December 16, 2006. Retrieved February 21, 2008 (http://www.nytimes.com/2006/12/16/health/16iodine.html).

Myers, Drew. "Chemistry of Photography." The Chemical Engineers' Resource Page. Retrieved February 23, 2008 (http://www.cheresources.com/photochem.shtml).

National Oceanic and Atmospheric Administration. "Cloud Seeding." Retrieved February 21, 2008 (http://www.aoml.noaa.gov/hrd/nhurr97/CSEED.HTM).

Rovner, Sophie. "Cool Currency Facts." June 11, 2007. Retrieved February 23, 2008 (http://pubs.acs.org/cen/science/85/8524sci1a.html).

The Science Teacher. "Ground Level Ozone Testing." December 1995. Retrieved February 23, 2008 (http://teachertech.rice.edu/participants/lee/tropo.html).

Seppa, Nathan. "Thyroid Cancer Rose After Chernobyl." *Science News*, Vol. 156.6. August 7, 1999, p. 95. Retrieved January 30, 2008 (http://find.galegroup.com/itx/start.do?prodId=ITOF).

Stwertka, Albert. *A Guide to the Elements*. 2nd ed. New York, NY: Oxford University Press, 2002.

United Press International. "White House Drops Anti-Radiation Pill Plan." January 29, 2008. Retrieved February 23, 2008 (http://www.upi.com/NewsTrack/Top_News/2008/01/29/white_house_drops_anti-radiation_pill_plan/5178).

U.S. Environmental Protection Agency. "Emergency Disinfection of Drinking Water." November 28, 2006. Retrieved February 23, 2008 (http://epa.gov/ogwdw/faq/emerg.html).

About the Author

Kristi Lew is a professional K–12 educational writer with degrees in biochemistry and genetics. A former high school science teacher, she specializes in writing textbooks, magazine articles, and nonfiction books about science, health, and the environment for students and teachers.

Photo Credits

Designer: Tahara Anderson; Editor: Kathy Kuhtz Campbell
Photo Researcher: Marty Levick